811
LEE

Lee, Dennis.

79181

Dinosaur dinner with
a slice of alligator
pie : favorite poems

$20.51

DATE DUE	BORROWER'S NAME	ROOM NO.

79181

811
LEE

Lee, Dennis.

Dinosaur dinner with
a slice of alligator
pie : favorite poems

SISKIYOU CO OFFICE ED/LIBRARY

Favorite Poems by
Dennis Lee

Dinosaur
Dinner

(With a Slice of Alligator Pie)

Selected by
Jack Prelutsky

Illustrated by
Debbie Tilley

Alfred A. Knopf
New York

For Jake
—D. L.

For Stephen Gould
—D. T.

http://www.randomhouse.com/

Grateful acknowledgment is made to Scholastic, Inc., for permission to reprint "Big Bad Billy," "The Butterfly,"
"The Ice Cream Store," "I'm Not Coming Out," "Lucy Go Lightly," "Mabel," "Mrs. Mitchell's Underwear,"
"The Perfect Pets," "Peter Ping and Patrick Pong," and "The Secret Place" from *The Ice Cream Store*
by Dennis Lee. Copyright © 1991 by Dennis Lee. Reprinted by special permission of Scholastic, Inc.
The other poems in this work were originally published in Canada by Macmillan Canada in the following collections:
Alligator Pie (1974), *Garbage Delight* (1977), and *Jelly Belly* (1983).

Library of Congress Cataloging-in-Publication Data
Lee, Dennis, 1939–
Dinosaur dinner with a slice of alligator pie: favorite poems / by Dennis Lee ; selected by Jack Prelutsky ;
illustrated by Debbie Tilley.
p.   cm.
Summary: An illustrated collection of humorous poems on a variety of topics.
1. Children's poetry, Canadian. [1. Humorous poetry. 2. Canadian poetry.] I. Prelutsky, Jack. II. Tilley, Debbie, ill.
III. Title.
PR9199.3.L387D56   1997
811'.54—dc20 96-31100

ISBN 0-679-87009-1 (trade)
ISBN 0-679-97009-6 (lib. bdg.)

Printed in the United States of America

10 9 8 7 6 5 4 3 2

The Dinosaur Dinner

Allosaurus, Stegosaurus,
Brontosaurus too,
All went off for dinner at the
Dinosaur zoo;

Along came the waiter, called
Tyrannosaurus Rex,
Gobbled up the table
'Cause they wouldn't pay their checks.

Mabel

Mabel dear,
It's not a stable:
Take your front legs
Off the table,

Place your hooves
Upon the floor,
And do not whinny
Anymore.

Alligator Pie

Alligator pie, alligator pie,
If I don't get some I think I'm gonna die.
Give away the green grass, give away the sky,
But don't give away my alligator pie.

Alligator stew, alligator stew,
If I don't get some I don't know what I'll do.
Give away my furry hat, give away my shoe,
But don't give away my alligator stew.

Alligator soup, alligator soup,
If I don't get some I think I'm gonna droop.
Give away my hockey stick, give away my hoop,
But don't give away my alligator soup.

Three Tickles

Pizza, pickle,
Pumpernickel,
My little guy
Shall have a tickle:

One for his nose,
And one for his toes,
And one for his tummy
Where the hot dog goes.

Anna Banana

Anna Banana, jump into the stew:
Gravy and carrots are *good* for you.
Good for your teeth,
And your fingernails too,
So Anna Banana, jump into the stew!

I Eat Kids Yum Yum!

A child went out one day.
She only went to play.
A mighty monster came along
And sang its mighty monster song:

"I EAT KIDS YUM YUM!
I STUFF THEM DOWN MY TUM.
I ONLY LEAVE THE TEETH AND CLOTHES.
(I SPECIALLY LIKE THE TOES.)"

The child was not amused.
She stood there and refused.
Then with a skip and a little twirl
She sang the song of a hungry girl:

"I EAT MONSTERS BURP!
THEY MAKE ME SQUEAL AND SLURP.
IT'S TIME TO CHOMP AND TAKE A CHEW—
AND WHAT I'LL CHEW IS YOU!"

The monster ran like that!
It didn't stop to chat.
(The child went skipping home again
And ate her brother's model train.)

Tricking

When they bring me a plate
Full of stuff that I hate,
Like spinach and turnips and guck,
I sit very straight
And I look at the plate
And I quietly say to it: "YUCK!"

Little kids bawl
'Cause I used to be small,
And I threw it all over the tray.
But now I am three
And I'm much more like me—
I yuck till they take it away.

But sometimes my dad
Gets ter*riff*ickly mad,
And he says, "Don't you drink from that cup!"
But he can't say it right
'Cause he's not very bright—
So I trick him and drink it all up!

Then he gets up and roars;
He stomps on the floor
And he hollers, "I warn you, don't eat!!"
He counts up to ten
And I trick him again:
I practically finish the meat.

Then I start on the guck
And my daddy goes "Yuck!"
And he scrunches his eyes till they hurt!
So I shovel it in
And he grins a big grin.
And then we have dessert.

The Muddy Puddle

I am sitting
In the middle
Of a rather Muddy
Puddle,
With my bottom
Full of bubbles
And my rubbers
Full of Mud,

While my jacket
And my sweater
Go on slowly
Getting wetter
As I very
Slowly settle
To the Bottom
Of the Mud.

And I find that
What a person
With a puddle
Round his middle
Thinks of mostly
In the muddle
Is the Muddi-
Ness of Mud.

Dickery Dean

"What's the matter
    With Dickery Dean?
He jumped right into
    The washing machine!"

"Nothing's the matter
    With Dickery Dean—
He dove in dirty,
    And he jumped out clean!"

Mrs. Mitchell's Underwear

Mrs. Mitchell's underwear
    Is dancing on the line;
Mrs. Mitchell's underwear
    Has never looked so fine.

Mrs. Mitchell hates to dance—
    She says it's not refined,
But Mrs. Mitchell's underwear
    Is prancing on the line.

With a polka-dotted polka
    And a tangled tango too,
Mrs. Mitchell's underwear
    Is like a frilly zoo!

Catching

The boys catch the girls
And the girls catch the boys:
Kissing in the schoolyard,
What a yucky noise!

Double-barreled Ding-dong-bat

Why,
You—

Double-barreled,
Disconnected,
Supersonic
Ding-dong-bat:

Don't you dare come
Near me, or I'll
Disconnect you
Just like that!

Tony Baloney

Tony Baloney is fibbing again—
Look at him wiggle and try to pretend.
Tony Baloney is telling a lie:
Phony old Tony Baloney, goodbye!

Dirty Georgie

Georgie's face was
Never clean.
Georgie smelled like
Gasoline.

Kissing Georgie—
Mighty fine!
Just like kissing
Frankenstein!

Georgie, Georgie,
Wash your face,
Or we'll kick you out
Of the human race:

Not because you're ugly,
Not because you're cute,
Just because your dirty ears
Smell like rubber boots!

Mrs. Murphy and Mrs. Murphy's Kids

Mrs. Murphy,
     If you please,
Kept her kids
     In a can of peas.

The kids got bigger
     And the can filled up,
So she moved them into
     A measuring cup.

But the kids got bigger
     And the cup got crammed,
So she poured them into
     A frying pan.

But the kids grew bigger
     And the pan began to stink,
So she pitched them all
     In the kitchen sink.

But the kids kept growing
     And the sink went *kaplooey*,
So she dumped them on their ears
     In a crate of chop suey.

But the kids kept growing
     And the crate got stuck,
So she carted them away
     In a ten-ton truck.

And she said, "Thank goodness
     I remembered that truck,
Or my poor little children
     Would be out of luck!"

But the darn kids grew
     Till the truck wouldn't fit,
And she had to haul them off
     To a gravel pit.

But the kids kept growing
>Till the pit was too small,
So she bedded them down
>In a shopping mall.

But the kids grew enormous
>And the mall wouldn't do,
So she herded them together
>In an empty zoo.

But the kids grew gigantic
>And the fence went *pop!*
So she towed them away
>To a mountain top.

But the kids just grew
>And the mountain broke apart,
And she said, "Darned kids,
>They were pesky from the start!"

So she waited for a year,
>And she waited for another,
And the kids grew up
>And had babies like their mother.

And Mrs. Murphy's kids—
>You can think what you please—
Kept all *their* kids
>In a can of peas.

Skyscraper

Skyscraper, skyscraper,
Scrape me some sky:
Tickle the sun
While the stars go by.

Tickle the stars
While the sun's climbing high,
Then skyscraper, skyscraper,
Scrape me some sky.

Windshield Wipers

Windshield wipers
Wipe away the rain,
Please bring the sunshine
Back again.

Windshield wipers
Clean our car,
The fields are green
And we're traveling far.

My father's coat is warm.
My mother's lap is deep.
Windshield wipers
Carry me to sleep.

And when I wake,
The sun will be
A golden home
Surrounding me;

But if that rain
Gets worse instead,
I want to sleep
Till I'm in my bed.

Windshield wipers
Wipe away the rain,
Please bring the sunshine
Back again.

Little Miss Dimble

Little Miss Dimble
Lived in a thimble,
Slept in a measuring spoon.
She met a mosquito
And called him "My sweet-o,"
And married him under the moon.

The Butterfly

Butterfly,
  butterfly,
life's a
  dream;

all that we
  see,
and all that we
  seem,

here for a
  jiffy
and then
  goodbye—

butterfly,
  butterfly,
flutter
  on by.

Lucy Go Lightly

Lucy go lightly
  Wherever you go,
Light as a lark
  From your head to your toe;

In slippers you float
  And in sandals you flow—
So Lucy, go lightly
  Wherever you go.

The Bear and the Bees

Wiggle waggle went the bear,
Catching bees in his underwear.
  One bee out,
  And one bee in,
  And one bee bit him
  On his big bear skin.

Up in North Ontario

Up in North Ontario
A barber met a bear-io
And cut his curly hair-io,
Up in North Ontario.

Torontosaurus Rex

Torontosaurus Rex,
Torontosaurus Rex—
Tiny in the brain, but
Enormous in the neck.

Taller than the CN Tower,
Bigger than Quebec:
Don't fool around with
Torontosaurus Rex!

Ookpik

An Ookpik is nothing but hair.
If you shave him, he isn't there.

He's never locked in the zoo.
He lives in a warm igloo.

He can whistle and dance on the walls.
He can dance on Niagara Falls.

He has nothing at all on his mind.
If you scratch him, he wags his behind.

He dances from morning to night.
Then he blinks. That turns out the light.

Peter Was a Pilot

Peter was a pilot,
He flew a jumbo jet,
He crashed in Lake Ontario
And got his bottom wet.

Billy Batter

Billy Batter,
What's the matter?
How come you're so sad?
I lost my cat
In the laundromat,
And a dragon ran off with my dad,
My dad—
A dragon ran off with my dad!

Billy Batter,
What's the matter?
How come you're so glum?
I ripped my jeans
On the Coke machine,
And a monster ran off with my mum,
My mum—
A monster ran off with my mum!

Billy Batter,
Now you're better—
Happy as a tack!
The dragon's gone
To Saskatchewan;
The monster fell
In a wishing well;
The cat showed up
With a newborn pup;
I fixed the rips
With potato chips,
And my dad and my mum came back,
Came back—
My dad and my mum came back.

Mumbo, Jumbo

Mumbo   Jumbo
Christopher Colombo
I'm sitting on the sidewalk
Chewing bubble gumbo.

I think I'll catch a WHALE . . .
I think I'll catch a *snail* . . .
I think I'll sit around awhile
Twiddling my thumbo.

Doctor, Doctor

Doctor, Doctor, fix my head:
I'm feeling sick and I'll soon be dead!

Little girl, little girl, drink some juice:
You think too much and your brain's come loose.

Doctor, Doctor, here's a dime:
You saved my life for the forty-second time.

The Dreadful Doings of Jelly Belly

Jelly Belly bit
    With a big fat bite.
Jelly Belly fought
    With a big fat fight.

Jelly Belly scowled
    With a big fat frown.
Jelly Belly yelled
    Till his house fell down.

Peter Ping and Patrick Pong

When Peter Ping met Patrick Pong
They stared like anything.
For Ping (in fact) looked more like Pong,
While Pong looked more like Ping.

The reason was, a nurse had changed
Their cribs, and got them wrong—
So no one knew, their whole lives through,
That Pong was Ping; Ping, Pong.

Big Bad Billy

Big bad Billy
Had a button on his tum.

Big bad Billy
Said, "I'm gonna have some fun!"

Big bad Billy
Gave a tug, and then a shout—

And big bad Billy
Pulled his belly button out!

Willoughby Wallaby Woo

Willoughby, wallaby, woo.
I don't know what to do.

Willoughby, wallaby, wee.
An elephant sat on me.

Willoughby, wallaby, wash.
I'm feeling kind of squash.

Willoughby, wallaby, woo.
And I don't know what to do.

I Found a Silver Dollar

I found a silver dollar,
But I had to pay the rent.
I found an alligator
But his steering wheel was bent.
I found a little monkey,
So I took him to the zoo.
Then I found a sticky kiss and so
I brought it home to you.

The Perfect Pets

WAAAAL—
I had a *dog*,
And his name was Doogie,
And I don't know why
But he liked to boogie;

He boogied all night
He boogied all day
He boogied in a rude
Rambunctious way.

SOOOO—
I got a *cat*,
And her name was Bing,
And I don't know why
But she liked to sing;

She sang up high
She sang down deep
She sang like the dickens
When I tried to sleep.

SOOOO—
I got a *fox*,
And her name was Knox,
And I don't know why
But she liked to box;

She boxed me out
She boxed me in
She boxed me *smack!*
On my chinny-chin-chin.

Soooo—

I got a *grizzly*,
And his name was Gus,
And I don't know why
But he liked to fuss;

He fussed in the sun
He fussed in the rain
He fussed till he drove me
Half insane!

Nowwww—

I don't *know*,
But I've been told
That some people's pets
Are good as gold.

But there's Doogie and there's Bing,
And there's Knox and Gus,
And they boogie and they sing
And they box and fuss;

So I'm giving them away
And I'm giving them for free—
If you want a perfect pet,
Just call on me.

The Ice Cream Store

Oh, the kids around the block are like an
     Ice cream store,
'Cause there's chocolate, and vanilla,
     And there's maple and there's more,

And there's butterscotch and orange—
     Yes, there's flavors by the score;
And the kids around the block are like an
     Ice cream store!

Being Five

I'm not exactly big,
        And I'm not exactly little,
But being Five is best of all
        Because it's in the middle.

A person likes to ride his bike
        Around the block a lot,
And being Five is big enough
        And being Four is not.

And then he likes to settle down
        And suck his thumb a bit,
And being Five is small enough,
        But when you're Six you quit.

I've thought about it in my mind—
        Being Five, I mean—
And why I like it best of all
        Is 'cause it's In Between.

The Secret Place

There's a place I go, inside myself,
    Where nobody else can be,
And none of my friends can tell it's there—
    Nobody knows but me.

It's hard to explain the way it feels,
    Or even where I go.
It isn't a place in time or space,
    But once I'm there, I *know*.

It's tiny, it's shiny, it can't be seen,
    But it's big as the sky at night . . .
I try to explain and it hurts my brain,
    But once I'm there, it's *right*.

There's a place I know inside myself,
    And it's neither big nor small,
And whenever I go, it feels as though
    I never left at all.

I'm Not Coming Out

Cover me over
With blankets in bed:
A sheet on my feet
And a quilt on my head,

A frown on my face
And a pout on my snout—
I'm sad, and I'm mad,
And I'm not coming out!

And I don't care if they tickle,
And I don't care if they tease;
I don't care if they beg me to
Until their bottoms freeze,

'Cause it isn't very funny
When a person feels this way,
And it won't be very funny
If a person runs away.

So I'm not coming out, and I'm *not* coming out,
And I'm NOT coming out—and then,
They'll tell me that they're sorry . . .
And I *might* come out again.

The Ghost and Jenny Jemima

(slow and spooky)

The clock struck one,
The clock struck two,
The ghost came playing
Peekaboo.
> *Wa-ooo!*
> *Wa-ooo!*

The clock struck three,
The clock struck four,
And Jenny Jemima
Began to roar.
> *Wa-ooo!*
> *Wa-ooo!*

The clock struck five,
The clock struck six,
The ghost could walk through
Steel and bricks.
> *Wa-ooo!*
> *Wa-ooo!*

The clock struck seven,
The clock struck eight,
And Jenny Jemima's
Hair stood straight.
> *Wa-ooo!*
> *Wa-ooo!*

The clock struck nine,
The clock struck ten . . .
The ghost wound the clock,
And went home again.

(THE END)

The Gentle Giant

Every night
At twelve o'clock,
The gentle giant
Takes a walk;
With a cry cried high
And a call called low,
The gentle giant
Walks below.

And as he walks,
He cries, he calls:

"*Bad men, boogie men,*
Bully men, shoo!
No one in the neighborhood
Is scared of you.
The children are asleep,
And the parents are too:
Bad men, boogie men,
Bully men, shoo!"

Silverly

Silverly,
  Silverly,
Over the
  Trees
The moon drifts
  By on a
Runaway
  Breeze.

Dozily,
  Dozily,
Deep in her
  Bed,
A little girl
  Dreams with the
Moon in her
  Head.